The Aquinas Lecture, 1963

RELIGION AND ART

Under the Auspices of Wisconsin-Alpha
Chapter of the Phi Sigma Tau

by

PAUL WEISS, Ph.D.

MARQUETTE UNIVERSITY PRESS
MILWAUKEE
1963

Library of Congress Catalog Card Number: 63-13170

PRINTED IN U.S.A.

To Mortimer Adler

Prefatory

The Wisconsin-Alpha Chapter of Phi Sigma Tau, the National Honor Society for Philosophy at Marquette University, each year invites a scholar to deliver a lecture in honor of St. Thomas Aquinas, whose feast day is March 7. These lectures are called the Aquinas Lectures, and are customarily given on the second Sunday of March.

In 1963 the Aquinas Lecture "Religion and Art" was delivered on March 10 in the Peter A. Brooks Memorial Union of Marquette University by Dr. Paul Weiss, Sterling Professor of philosophy, Yale University.

Professor Weiss was born in New York City's lower East Side on May 19, 1901. Before he could graduate from high school, circumstances required that he earn his own living. Six years later he returned to the evening division of New York City College, then transferred to the regular college program and received his A.B. degree in 1927 and was elected to Phi Beta Kappa. He received his M.A. degree from Harvard in 1928 and his Ph.D. in 1929. After a year as research fellow in philosophy in Germany and France, he taught at Harvard and then Bryn Mawr. In 1945 he was visiting professor at Yale and the following year became a permanent member of the faculty.

Professor Weiss has played an important role in promoting the exchange of philosophical ideas. He is the founder of The Metaphysical Society of America, and of the Philosophy Education Society, Inc.; founder and editor of the *Review of Metaphysics;* and a founding member of the Conference of Science, Philosophy and Religion. In addition, he has served on the Executive Committee of the American Philosophical Association and the Symbolic Logic Association; and on the Editorial Board of *Science of Culture* and *Judaism;* is a trustee of the American Association of Middle East Studies and is consultant for the Great Books Program, and for the Institute for Philosophical Research. He gave the William Powell Lectures at the University of Indiana in 1958.

His published works include: *The Modes of Being* (Carbondale: Southern Illinois University Press, 1958); *Man's Freedom* (New Haven: Yale University Press, 1950); *Reality* (Princeton: Princeton University Press, 1938; Gloucester: Peter Smith, 1949); *Nature and Man* (New York: Henry Holt, 1947); *Our Public Life* (Bloomington: University of Indiana Press, 1959); *The World of Art* (Carbondale: Southern Illinois University Press, 1961); *Nine Basic Arts* (Carbondale: Southern Illinois University Press, 1961); *History: Written and Lived* (Carbondale: Southern Illinois University Press, 1962).

He is co-editor of the six-volume: *The Collected Works of Charles Sanders Peirce*; and co-author of *Philosophical Essays of A. N. Whitehead; American Philosophy, Today and Tomorrow*; *Science, Philosophy and Religion*; *Approaches to World Peace*; *Freedom and Reason*; *Moral Principles of Action*; *Moments of Personal Discovery*, and others.

To these books and many articles in learned journals Phi Sigma Tau has the pleasure of adding *Religion and Art*.

Religion and Art

I

All basic enterprises have at least seven important relations to one another. Religion and art are no exception. (a) They are independent, each providing an answer to man's basic need to be perfected. Each can have the other as a subdivision, to yield (b) sacramental works, art in the service of religion, and (c) secularized religion, religion as a subdivision of art. Each can also be completed by the other. Consecrated art is art completed by religion (d), whereas (e) liturgical art is religion completed by art. Finally, we have (f) religion as ceremonial, religion qualified by art, and (g) religious art, art religiously qualified. I will concentrate on the last of these, but some attention must be paid to the others.

II

(a) *The Claims of Religion and Art:* Religious men, again and again, have yielded to the power of the state and the lures of other pursuits. But there have also been religious men who have resisted these. In every generation some men seem to maintain a firm faith in God, no matter what happens with nations or states, and no matter what promises are offered by inquiry, other men, or art. Alert to the fact that they occupy themselves with a being greater than any to be encountered elsewhere, they rightly insist on the fact that religion cannot, without mutilation, be subordinated to any other enterprise. They tend, in fact, to insist that other disciplines should be subordinated and guided by religion. Sometimes an attempt is made to bolster the insistence with the argument that religion is superior to other enterprises, because it is not only concerned with a superior object but also enables a man to achieve the highest possible good. Philosophers are sometimes admonished to deal with God first, because God is the first of beings; ethicists are told to begin with God's commands because His commands override all others; artists are urged to occupy themselves with religious topics for they then will benefit from the best of ultimate realities. The recommendations, I think, have little to recommend them.

An enterprise which is concerned with madness or ugliness or sickness is not necessarily mad, ugly or sick, nor is it necessarily inferior to those which deal with sanity, beauty, or health. An enterprise which concerns itself with the first or best of things is not necessarily the first or the best of enterprises. The study may not be properly geared to the superior being; also, that being could be outside the reach of any agency that a man could employ; and immersion in some other activity might be necessary before one could be in a position to deal properly with the best of beings.

There are, as a matter of fact, multiple needs which must be taken care of before

God could be properly faced. These do and ought to come before a concern with God, both in time and in principle. Without them there would be no way of having a satisfactory concern for God. A man who neither eats, drinks, sleeps, thinks, or acts is not long for this world, and while he is in it, will soon be too weak to do much justice to the onerous demands of a rich and well-focussed faith. Even if it were true that an inquiry or code should first deal with God, it may not be true that the greatest good will thereupon accrue to man. Religion nurtures fanatics as well as saints, bigots as well as men of peace, foolish men and wise ones.

Religion is not a light matter. It can do irreparable harm. To engage in it properly one must be mature, sane, judicious, and strong, or be kept in place by others who are. Those who are not religious, or not vigorously so, soon learn to be wary of some full believers. Sooner or later it is found that rights, privileges, opportunities, and insights are denied in the name of God.

Claims on behalf of religion are in fact countered by equally insistent claims made on behalf of art, as well as by other enterprises. Art refuses to be completely subordinated to religion, or to anything else. Indeed, it could not yield to them without becoming hobbled or distorted. It can be properly pursued only by one who gives himself fully to it. And he could, with some plausibility, urge that everything else, including religion, give way to it. Art, after all, expresses man at his most creative; it exposes his deepest secrets and thereby enables him to know himself; it purifies and refreshes him; it confronts him with an irreplaceable beauty and makes him aware of what the world promises him and the rest of mankind. Still, art does not provide men with all the goods they need—any more than religion or any other enterprise does.

Art does not, cannot replace religion, ethics, or inquiry, for it cannot yield the goods that come when one has faith, lives up to his obligations, or uses his intellect in order to learn. Sometimes art quickens uncontrollable passions. It can provoke thoughts and feelings which endanger the continuance of established and desirable ways. Precisely because it is and ought to be pursued wholeheartedly, art risks running afoul of the truths and rights which religion, ethics, and knowledge defend, exhibit, and promote. The free creativity which art requires affects men who do not have the power to keep it within the grooves, which would allow them to live together in tranquility and to attend to what transcends the world where men create. The artist, too, has obligations to fulfill, a final assessment to face, and a mind to exercise. He must make room for other kinds of dedications besides his own.

Both religion and art have distinctive rights. Each justifiably urges itself as a primary discipline. Each provides goods that are obtainable nowhere else. To have one of these enterprises and not the other is to have less than one ought and can have. Yet no one can engage in both fully. Religion demands too much of a man's time, attention, energies, and decisions to make it possible for him to devote himself to art as much as a man ought. The reverse is true as well. A life dedicated to art allows an insufficient place for religion, if religion is to be taken with the seriousness it deserves. There have, of course, been religious men who have distinguished themselves in painting, music, and poetry as well as in other arts, and there have been artists who have made religion a matter of primary concern. But these men did not somehow make themselves double; instead they occupied themselves with sacramental, consecrated, or religious arts, with secularized religion, liturgical arts, or with ceremony and ritual. They did not deal fully with both religion and art as independent, distinctive enterprises. They could not do so except by living two lives in one life span.

No man, by himself, can do all a man ought to do in order to live a full life. Some of the goods he needs can be obtained only by his devoting himself to one course and slighting others where equally important goods are to be obtained. All men necessarily lead partial lives. But no one need be content with only those goods that he individually can obtain. Each can benefit from the work others do. While engaged in the pursuit of one discipline he can make himself receptive to the goods that other disciplines provide. He can take men engaged in other disciplines to represent him in somewhat the way we all take policemen and senators, priests and soldiers, diplomats and athletes to be acting on our behalf. Ideally, each man contributes to a common treasury of goods to be shared in equally by everyone. All men trod a narrow path, but together they can win for all the goods each requires.

A man can spend himself either in a religious life or in a life devoted to art. He will then live as he ought—provided that he takes the goods produced in the other area to be no less accreditable to himself than those which he himself has won, and, of course, also provided that he takes the goods he brought about to be no more accreditable to himself than the goods others are responsible for. The religious man should acknowledge, not reject the goods that are obtained by those who turn away from the religious life; the artist should acknowledge, not reject the goods that are obtained by those who neglect the world of art. Both should attend to the accomplishments of others who spend their lives in other ways—and conversely.

The acceptance of values obtained through the pursuit of other disciplines is to be sharply distinguished from the use of the works produced in those other disciplines. The former demands that the disciplines continue to be independent in act and being, the latter requires their reduction to the position of components in some more inclusive enterprise. Religion can benefit from the fact that there are men who are wholeheartedly devoted to the independent production of beauty; art can benefit from the fact that there are men who are wholeheartedly devoted to promoting a rich, final assessment to which all men will be subject. The addition of partial lives and values adds up to a full life, a totality of value.

Both religion and art will suffer if they allow themselves to be merged or used as supplements of one another, unless they continue at the same time to be pursued as basic, independent enterprises. Adding the distinctive works of one venture to those of another brings their different criteria and demands into conflict, where it does not blur their edges, spoil their aims and destroy their autonomy. There is no place for paintings or sculpture in a synagogue or a mosque; religions unduly constrain the creative dancer and the rebellious poet. There is no time for prayer or meditation when one is caught up in the process of creativity; arts turn the attention away from the centre of religious faith.

Art is not only to be pursued independently of religion; it can and it ought to be subject to religion. Religion is not only to be pursued independently of art, but it can and ought to be subject to art. Each is in fact a basic discipline only so far as it is able to subordinate all else. Art and religion are not only independent of one another, but provide a place within themselves, both for one another and for the other basic disciplines. So far as it is included in another, it will of course no longer be as it was when independently pursued; it will then have material, media, objectives, conditions, and criteria in part dictated by what encompasses it.

III

(b) *Sacramental Works:* There are areas in all religions where gracefulness, beauty, and aesthetic qualities are particularly dominant. These do not offer us instances of art, however. They are parts, subdivisions of religion, media, agencies, instruments for the exercise or stimulation of it. Religion provides an occasion for them; it may provide the topics and state the conditions to which the workers in these areas must conform. They are sacramental works—sometimes loosely called sacramental arts. Not produced as works of art, not dealt with as works of art, they are at best excellent works of craftsmanship or excellent instruments for the promotion of religion.

A psalm, a chant, a poem, a candelabra, an altar, even a cathedral may be only a sacramental work, and not reach the status of an art. One can, of course, isolate any one of these and work over it in terms of criteria and for objectives of a purely aesthetic nature. This seems often to have been done. But then the work is taken out of its religious context and dealt with as an object of a secular art, or as the product of a religious art. If reinserted into a religious context, it will once again function as an instrument, to be used, manipulated, passed through, not enjoyed for the beauty it embodies or the light it throws on turbulent existence, with its veiled promise of good and evil—which is to say, it will not, so far, be dealt with as a work of art.

A sacramental work need not have any religious content or reference. It is enough that its excellence serve the purpose of a religion. It retains its obtrusive features—it continues to be well-made—while it promotes the ends of religion.

Sacramental works are at once excellent and efficacious. What is not both is not a sacramental work. This means that some works of art and some effective instruments are not sacramental works. Not every work of art of great distinction provides a good occasion for carrying out a religious purpose. Some are too upsetting. They involve the passions too much; they enrapture, turning one away from religious matters. They are not sacramental works. Picasso's "Guernica" offers a good illustration. Though it has been praised by Tillich as a work of art which is truly religious, on the rather strange grounds that it points up the evils of our time and the anxieties these entrain, it is, in fact, a work of art of little if any religious significance. If it makes us think of war and its horrors, and of possible divine reasons or remedies for these, it still does not function as a sacramental work or as a work of religious art. A sacramental work must serve the purposes of religion; a work of religious art must express a religious faith, bear the marks of the presence of God. If the "Guernica" does these things it does so incidentally, adventitiously, by "accident."

What awakens a thought or an interest in God is not necessarily something religious. To be religious it must awaken the thought or interest within a religious context, where a faith is being exercised. Inside a religion, however, there are activities and objects, long-hallowed by tradition, which are poorly organized, often ugly and in poor taste, and yet which are most efficacious in promoting the religion. Since they lack excellence they fall short of being sacramental works. On the other hand, it is possible to view a work of art, even the "Guernica," within the framework of some religion, and find that it sustains and enriches religious activity, particularly by means of the beauty it embodies. But it will then so far not function as a work of art, religious or secular, since its role as art object will have been passed over to make it serve a nonaesthetic purpose. When works of art are bought and sold, used to hide ugly walls, approved because of their propagandistic, educative, or therapeutic value, a similar neglect of their status as works of art is involved.

All religions aschew some works of art. They all know with Plato that some works represent dangers for the established order, and will more likely than not corrupt or misdirect those who are most sensitive to them. Some religious men think all art endangers religion and should be rigidly controlled or perhaps even totally suppressed. Practice wisely defies such men, even when they are able to achieve positions of power, or manage to get their opinions written into creeds or ordinances. The religious efficacy of some works well-made is too striking to allow for the wholesale condemnation of art by religious men.

If a religion forbids the making of images, recourse will be had to music, arabesques, dance; if it forbids the use of song, men will cultivate the graces of speech; if it frowns on the theatre or the use of musical instruments, it will allow room for architecture or poetry. Could it set itself against all forms of artistic expression, it would not only deny men the right to make excellently, but would deny itself opportunities to flourish. No discipline, no matter how glorious its object, has the right to oppose strong impulses on the part of men to make excellently. Nor would any succeed in opposing such impulses for long —nor in the end would it benefit from the result.

From the standpoint of religion, the most important thing about a work is its efficacy in promoting the religion. Some among the efficacious instruments for religion will be excellently made, but that excellence may not have relevance for the efficacy. The excellence will then be useless and perhaps even distracting. So far as the religion is concerned, precisely because it is a work the appreciation of whose excellence takes time and attention from and so far precludes the practice of the religion, the work is to be opposed by the religion. Only in those cases where the excellence of a work contributes toward the effective participation in the religion is it to be welcomed by the religion.

Because no one can tell in advance just which excellent works will be in consonance with the best spirit of a religion, no one who makes religion his primary concern can encourage the free pursuit of art. There are men who would contest this view. They think that religion has an omnivorous appetite for whatever is good. According to them, religion opposes no worthwhile expression, no product of human endeavor, providing it be backed by sincerity, ability, and control. The facts are against them. Of course, eventually a religion should accommodate all goods. But this it cannot do until it is at its best. That means it must first withstand the temptations presented by various excellencies pursued in nonreligious contexts.

Once a religion has attained the stage where, without losing focus, it is receptive to whatever goods there be, it can turn about and accept what it had put aside, but only on the condition that the excellencies be treated as instances or fragments of the excellence embodied in the religion. A great work of art which had been put aside because it did not promote or because it in fact hindered the pursuit of the religion, would then be dealt with as providing a signal instance of what can be achieved by men in the beneficent presence of God. It would not be lived with for its own sake, but would instead be accepted as an instance of a supposedly more comprehensive excellence, that of a firm faith. Enjoyed then as a great work of art, it will not yield an enjoyment identical with that obtained by one who approaches the work outside the religious context, where it is admired for what it is and conveys, and not for what it instances.

Different religious faiths need different types of support, encouragement, stimulation. Even apart from the particular imagery which is appropriate to one religion but not to another, they accept and oppose different excellent works, because and so far as these help or hinder them. Only he who accepts a religion and is concerned with strengthening it, is in a position to deal properly with the claims of various works to be accepted or at least tolerated by that religion. The issue is a practical one, and must be left in the hands of those who are required to make good practical decisions on behalf of a particular religion. A different kind of decision is required if we turn from the present question of art, viewed from the perspective of a religion, to the next question of religion, viewed from the perspective of art.

(c) *Secularized Religion:* Art recognizes no one's right to restrict its subject matter or the way it is to treat this. No one, not even the most pious of men, has the right to dictate to it. From its perspective, religion is a topic no less legitimate than any other.

An art might intensify, record, caricature, distort, or blur religion's activities and intent. When it does one of these things it is sometimes referred to as a religious art. Strictly speaking, though, as we shall see below, religious art has a being and a meaning apart from all these uses. It is a form of religion lived through in the course of the production of a work of beauty; but the cases we have just been considering are cases of art in which religion is used as an occasion, as material, or as topic.

Religious art embodies and points to

Existence as affected by God. The fact that it embodies and points to a divinely altered Existence distinguishes it from both secular art and pure religion. A secular art may portray religious figures, events, stories or gods, but only as an occasion to convey the nature of Existence as it stands outside and over against God. A pure religion may be expressed in beautiful songs and gestures, but these, like the song of a bird or the movement of a gazelle, are expressions of energies undirected, undisciplined, uncreated. They are natural beauties, not beauties made with art.

When religion is treated from the perspective of art, it is dealt with from the outside. It may then be beautified, aesthetically secularized. The result will contrast quite sharply not only with pure religion but with ceremonial religion (i.e., religion produced as a work of art) and with religious art (i.e., art as a form of religion). Pure religion, ceremonial religion, and religious art are all concerned with subject matters faced directly and not from alien perspectives. The first has to do with the exercise of a faith, the second with art, though one restricted to a limited area, and the third with a similarly restricted religion.

A beautified religion is an aesthetically secularized religion, a religion approached from the outside. The approach is legitimate. But it does affront some defenders of religion. We hear them complain that scientific, psychological, psycho-somatic or psycho-analytic, and other treatments of religion necessarily fall short of what religion is, what it intends, and what it accomplishes. We hear of objections to the study of comparative religion on the ground that only he who actually practices a religion, only he who deals with it from the inside of a complete conviction can know what a religion is or intends. Similar comments, however, could be made and are often made on behalf of other subject matters. Who but a biologist can say just what biology is, does, or even knows? Must not all sociological, psycho-analytic or other studies of biology and biologists fall short of it? Do not all philosophies of science, studies in scientific method, even biochemistry and biophysics necessarily stop at the edges of biology?

Nobody knows what a subject is on the inside but one who is on the inside. But all subjects have an outside as well, and that outside can be dealt with from many angles, all of which tell us something of what that outside is, and—unless the two are radically divorced—something of what the inside is like, as well.

Since an aesthetically secularized religion is religion dealt with from the perspective of art, one is more likely to misconstrue it if one misunderstands the nature of art than if one misunderstands the nature of religion. Those who see art as a tissue of ideas, propositions, feelings, symbolic forms, illusions and the like will inevitably treat an aesthetically secularized religion as more or less private, personal, in which nothing is made, nothing is objectively real.

Art is a basic enterprise because it provides an indispensable way of effectively dealing with Existence, the spatio-temporal dynamic cosmos of which we are now a part. We struggle with that Existence in many ways. It is encountered, faced as facing us, struggled with, interplayed with as having a career with which our own must be harmonized. If the encounter is overlooked, we will be led to suppose that Existence is not a reality, but rather an extension of man and his needs—or conversely, that men are but functions or foci of Existence. Personalists and existentialists tend to accept the first of these alternatives, materialists the second. Neither is tenable. If Existence has no reality apart from man, men could not live together nor keep apace in a public world. If men had no reality apart from Existence, they would not be able to defy, oppose, and act on it. We all stand over against Existence, and we all encompass a part of it within ourselves, thereby making ourselves present beings. There is of course, no time when we were nonexistents who laid hold of Existence to make it our own; we issue out of other limited existents, each of which has Existence within it. The existence of each of us is continuous with cosmic Existence; yet each of us stands over against that cosmic Existence, possessing our own fragment of that Existence in our own way.

Existence is extended; it is spatial, temporal, and dynamic. Each present actuality, because it has some Existence within it, is also spatial, temporal, and dynamic. As standing over against the whole of Existence, it forces Existence's space, time, and vitality into new shapes and gives them new careers. The space, time and vitality of Actualities are not altogether homogeneous with the space, time, and vitality characteristic of Existence. But since the existence of each Actuality is also a delimitation of the whole of Existence, the space, time, and vitality of each Actuality are continuous with that which lies outside. Existence pulls on the portion of existence which is encompassed by Actualities. Each Actuality, to continue to be in existence, must therefore adjust itself to Existence. If it succeeds, it keeps abreast of other Actualities in the same space, within a common time, through a common process of causation. If it fails, it becomes a bare fact, a past item, no longer present, lacking Existence.

The reality of a distinctive, possessed portion of Existence in each Actuality enables it to be at once continuous with and opposed to the Existence that remains outside. The continuity makes it possible for the Actuality to be a unit inside Existence, and to be subject to Existence's stresses and laws; the opposition makes it possible for the Actuality to impose itself on Existence, subject Existence to itself. In recent times, under the influence of Dewey and Wittgenstein, Anglo-Saxon philosophers have tended to insist on the former fact and to ignore the latter. But the two together are needed if there is to be an adjustment of Actualities to Existence, and thus a world in which beings, while living through their own careers, occupy a common field and mark out a common time.

Dewey on the whole is inclined to hold that individuals have some kind of being, and that they make some difference to what lies outside them, whereas Wittgenstein is inclined to hold that individuals are simple localizations of the world beyond, and that their main task is to fit inside it more snugly than they had. Dewey too seems to hold that we are indeterminate realities apart from that world and that that world is indeterminate apart from our response to it, whereas Wittgenstein seems to take the world to be fully determinate and we to be incapable of contributing anything to it.

Dewey's position is the stronger in one respect, and Wittgenstein's in another. We surely act on the world about, even when this is treated, as it is by Wittgenstein, as significant only when framed in a public language. This Dewey sees. But he cannot show why we should act on the world. Granted that we and the world are indeterminate, it still does not follow that we would want to, or that we would be able to do anything about it. One could be indeterminate in oneself or in a world for an indefinite period, and remain content with that state of affairs. We evidently have something to contribute to the world, and something to gain from it. But unless we knew where to go and what to do, we would continue to remain where and as we are.

On Wittgenstein's view we have nothing to contribute to the world about, for this apparently is fully determinate, absolutely meaningful, the locus of all values. Only he who is part of it can be meaningful, valuable. Wittgenstein thinks we ought to enter that world. But who is this who is to enter? What is there apart from the world on this view, but something completely amorphous, unintelligible, inaccessible? How could such a being know that it was desirable to enter that world? We must say either that the being never leaves it and never could leave it, never adds anything to it or takes anything away from it, or that the being is wholly passive and must be forced into it and pushed out of it. We do not seem to be able to say on this view that a man can enter into or leave the public world on his own terms.

Both these thinkers overlook the fact that a man has a nature, desires, objectives of his own, that he has determinations other than what the world contains or now accommodates, and that he tries to find a place for himself in that world, in the process of which he alters himself and that world to some degree.

Dewey is a democrat and a Darwinian, and seems to suppose that we are all engaged in a struggle to produce a new species of being, the well-adjusted man who moves smoothly through all situations, to reach the objects of his desires. Dewey is also a Hegelian, and in the end denies reality to anything which is not part of a final, substantial, perfect whole. Wittgenstein is a refugee whose students wish to belong to the upper strata of a caste society. Both he and they have good reasons for wanting to know the rules of the language "games" to which they can conform readily. He, reasonably enough, is concerned with the daily language used in the new country; they, as natives, have an equal warrant for being concerned with the upper class language of that country.

Wittgensteinians view language the

way amateurs view chess—as a set of rules one ought to follow, without reflection and without error. But the rules of a language, as well as the patterns of the richer world of reality, (part of which we use language to order, record, and communicate) ought not to be followed blindly, mechanically. They ought to be made part of oneself in such a way that they can be given different weights at different junctures. Our model should be, not amateurs but chess masters, who in effect constantly forge new rules in the very course of playing their games. The rules that amateurs learn and follow are not avoided or even changed by the experts. One plays correctly by following those rules. But one does not play well, until those rules are used as boundaries, limits, general guides to be quickened, re-evaluated, interlocked in different ways in different circumstances.

Each situation must be dealt with on its own merits. Dewey sees this but tends to speak as though each situation should be dealt with in isolation from others. He insists that we ought to make use of lessons previously learned and that we ought to keep our objective in view, but he does not see that each situation should be dealt with as part of a larger desirable whole, whose general outlines are already clear. He does not see that the nature and value of each situation should be determined in the light of that whole, the other steps that would be required, and the kind of opposition one might encounter.

We must avoid mere improvization, tactics without strategy, mere piecemeal answers. But we need not then go all the way to the opposite extreme and insist on a strategy without tactics, wholesale answers. We must deal with the particular situation but in the light of all else. We must adjust ourselves to whatever we encounter, in consonance with what we have already learned, the laws that prevail, the obstacles that we confront, and the promising openings we discern or see that we can bring about. But what we encounter insists on itself. Each insistence specifies a common insistence rooted in a reality which we can faintly discern lying beyond them, and enabling the specific insistencies to be interrelated and systematically dealt with. Each brute force specifies the compulsion of an ultimate Existence, to which we try to adjust ourselves in at least eight ways, of which one of the best is producing and sharing in works of art.

1) We are beings of habit, and Existence is somewhat regular in its activities. We quickly learn something of the cut of nature, of the way in which it performs, and we adjust our activities and attitudes to enable us to keep abreast of it. We survive because we know how to avoid the great dangers she offers, and we prosper because we know how to take advantage of her power and fruits. But we never know all the turns and twists of which she is capable; no set of habits, no attunement to what nature had been, will prevent us from being unprepared, devastated, overwhelmed at subsequent times. Sooner or later we must look to other remedies.

2) In the East more than in the West, but occasionally in the West as well, an attempt is made to adjust oneself to Ex-

istence by separating oneself from it. But this would seem to leave oneself open to an even more ready destruction and failure than would an habituated interplay with Existence. Precisely because Existence has its own independent and somewhat free development there can be no proper adjustment to it unless we allow ourselves to mesh with it, and do not stand over against it, rigidified by what we had previously learned from it. The followers of Tao say that if we relax, we will live in closer consonance with Existence than we would were we to make a concerted effort to deal with it, to impose our will or our desires on it. Still, it is a fact that there are cataclysms, sudden turns, threats, and compulsions which Existence imposes on us, no matter how relaxed we are.

3) The Stoic responds to this problem by taking the opposite tack from the preceding thinkers. He seeks to submit himself to Existence, to live in the light of its laws and nature. Since he supposes that it is essentially law-abiding and rational, he concludes that one who suppressed his

appetites and transcended everything peculiar, individual, and aberrant, would be perfectly adjusted to it. But nature is not as neatly organized as the Stoic tacitly takes it to be. There are accidents, unexpected surges, modifications, changes everywhere. No one who has made himself in consonance with nature's laws would be altogether in consonance with nature, and thus with the more inclusive Existence, in fact.

4) The Stoic outlook does, however, focus attention on the way of adjusting oneself to Existence which is characteristic of our modern epoch, the way of knowledge. In the sciences and in cosmology an attempt is made to understand the nature of the world. When we know, we take within ourselves the essence, the very meaning of what we know, and in this sense make it part of ourselves. We complete ourselves through knowledge, and when we know what Existence is, we possess it and therefore do not have it over against us as something wholly alien, opaque, and defiant. But this is true only

of the essence of Existence. Existence as a compulsive insistent realm is more than something which we have caught in knowledge. Nothing of it, to be sure, is intrinsically unknowable. But to say this is not the same thing as to say that our knowledge is identical with it. Our knowledge is a knowledge of it, all of it, a knowledge which nevertheless leaves it be over against us and our knowledge.

5) Our scientific knowledge does enable us to adjust ourselves to Existence when that knowledge is used instrumentally, as a guide and structure for the production and use of agencies of control. To master the forces about, we must achieve a technological control of them. This requires both a scientific understanding and an application of scientific knowledge to particular matters of fact. But Existence is vast, and any technological achievement is limited in scope and outcome. All our technical knowledge is geared in terms of general laws and stable ways; it cannot do full justice to the spontaneities and contingencies of what lies beyond us.

6) The foregoing devices for adjusting oneself to Existence are for the most part employed by individuals, though science and technology are of course pursued by a number working more or less in harmony. All of them occur in a society; they can even be said to be social products or social devices, presupposing a prior mastery of Existence in society.

A society is produced when a portion of Existence is separated out, and structured in new ways. Just so far as we adjust ourselves to society's ways, we necessarily so far adjust ourselves to Existence. And so far as the society itself, through the agency of its own habituations, retreats, advances, science and technology, is adjusted to the ways of Existence, we, in living in consonance with our society, will live in consonance with Existence itself. But no one of us fits perfectly inside his own society; each of us is in the process of helping constitute it, and of keeping abreast of it as constituted by others. And our society, precisely because its science and technology have a limited range, are framed in terms of universals, and face a domain which has multiple pivotal and idiosyncratic points and expressions, does not offer an adequate protection against a maladjustment to Existence.

7) History is the product of the interplay of man with Existence. It presupposes a prior interplay of man with a portion of Existence so as to constitute a society, a state or some organization of men. But unlike those who, in the spirit of the discussion in the preceding case, seek to live inside a society, those who participate in history are involved in an adjustment of groups of men, and eventually of mankind, to Existence, to achieve a kind of peace for themselves and eventually of mankind. But that peace is not yet and may never be. And this is perhaps as much as one can say about the outcome of man's struggle with Existence.

8) Art in a way unites all the previous ways in which one can adjust to Existence. It involves some grasp of Existence's contours, a turning away from it so that something can be made, a penetration into it

if only in intent, some understanding of its structure, a mastery of technology, an acceptance of society's way of possessing and facing that Existence, and a struggle with it. It masters Existence by representing it, by capturing it in a replica which reproduces Existence's texture and makes evident its import for us.

Art realizes a possible excellence in the form of beauty, by creatively working over recalcitrant material in such a way as to reproduce the texture of space, time, and becoming, and to make evident what bearing these in fact have on the promise of man. There is no material of which it may not make use; there are no absolutely unbreakable rules to which it must submit; there is no one order or direction it must follow; there is nothing which is necessarily excluded from its purview.

An atheist can paint a sensitive portrait of a rabbi or a priest. He can make a splendid set of Stations of the Cross, or a statue of a Buddha. He could design a prize-winning synagogue, church, or chapel. Books of merit can be written by men outside a faith about the men in it. In these cases religious men, their practices or their religion are taken to be material for an artistic production. The religion's nature is not affected. Rather, it is overlaid with other purposes, given new contexts, made to function in a nonreligious way. A more knowledgeable and sympathetic artist might not produce as good a work as an atheist, who is intent upon nothing but the best possible artistic production. There is, of course, no reason why such a knowledgeable and sympathetic artist might not produce an excellent work, using religious material, but whether he does or not, he will be occupied, not with religious matters, but with artistic ones. And, as we shall see below, it is possible for him to devote himself to producing a religious work of art which will bear the marks of the presence of God and refer to Him as qualifying Existence. No one but a religious man could produce such a religious work of art though it need not have a religious subject matter. A religious work of art may be produced out of any material and concern itself with any topic, but it must be made by a religious man.

There are evidently at least four distinct artistic products which should be distinguished: a secular work of art having a secular subject, a religious work of art having a secular subject, a secular work of art having a religious subject matter, and a religious work of art having a religious subject matter. A secular portrait of a politician makes evident, through the cues provided by the familiar or accepted delineaments of a political man, the nature of man and eventually of the Existence in which he shares and to which he is subject. A religious portrait of that very man done, let us say by the artist after he had been converted from one religion to another, or more sharply, from the status of an unbeliever to that of one who firmly and deeply believed along the lines of some one religion, might not be recognizably different from the secular portrait made earlier by that very artist—though this is not likely. To paint a religious portrait, even of a secular object, is to work at making evident God's presence throughout space, and thus His presence in and for the politician. If the portrait is indistinguishable from one excellently done in a secular spirit, it will, without losing its artistic excellence, be a poor religious work of art.

A secular artist who wishes to paint a portrait of a rabbi deals with a religious subject matter. The problems he faces as an artist are not different from those he faces when he paints a politician. Knowledge of religion is no more necessary for the one than a knowledge of politics is for the other. A religious portrait of a rabbi, on the other hand, if successfully done, will make evident the presence of God in and for the rabbi, and thereby in and for the whole of spatial Existence. Such a religious painting could be the work of a Christian or a Muslim, since it is concerned not with the distinctive Gods of the Christians, Muslims, or Jews, but with the God who will be evident to anyone who looks at the portrait with aesthetically sensitive eyes.

To the question of whether a Muslim

could be asked to compose a chant, design a church, make a crucifix, and the like, and then not as a craftsman, a skilled worker, but as an independent, creative artist, there should be an affirmative answer. If it is art that we want, the best artist should be employed, provided that he works as an artist. He will produce secular works if he concentrates only on capturing the texture and import of Existence in a sensuous form; he will produce religious works if he is attentive to the difference God makes to that Existence.

Superstitious beliefs and practices, idolatry, even atheism taken as a negative form of religion, can then be sympathetically portrayed by artists who have strong religious convictions. Such artists can be forbidden by their religions to engage themselves in these areas, just as they can be forbidden to make purely secular works of art. These prohibitions can be justified on the practical ground that they open faith to corruption or ridicule, encourage the practice of other religions, or draw the attention away from what should be at the centre. They cannot be justified by one who would take art seriously.

Whether the subject matter be secular or religious, a work could be religious. Consequently, if nothing be permitted but what promotes a given faith, art and the artist will be denied the opportunity to express religious truth in the way they can best do. That truth can be effectively conveyed through the avenue of nonreligious, areligious, and alien religious objects and practices. And whether the subject matter be secular or religious, the work could be a secular one. If nothing be permitted but what promotes a given faith, art and the artist will be denied the right to flourish, since this requires that they work in independence of religious needs.

Religion, when taken as the subject matter of art, may be so dealt with that a secular work results. The Bible can be read as literature, though it will then of course be treated as a secularized work whose religious utterances have been made subservient to the needs of art, in somewhat the same way as those utterances have been made subject to the exigencies of printing, binding, and marketing. There surely is no harm in this, providing it is not confused with or thought to replace other uses. Nor need one claim that the Bible is the best literature, or that it should serve as the model for all writers. Religious utterances are not necessarily the most amenable to the literary art, though of course there is no reason why this or that part of religion may not make the best possible material for an art. The stage, and the dance particularly, find it hard to make use of religious subject matter, and some religious events, such as the Crucifixion, have such an overwhelming emotional impact as to preclude all efforts at dramatization.

V

Religion can be made subject to art not only by being made a subject matter for it (c), but by being dealt with as material whose manipulation by an artist will help us grasp the import of Existence (e). It will then be correlative with (d) consecrated art, art offered up to God. Both of them (d and e) can be viewed as special cases of (f) religious ceremonial and of (g) religious art, the former making the practice of religion follow the demands of art, thereby revealing the import of Existence, the latter making art subject to religious conditions, thereby relating man to God. But it is worth noting that when religion is treated as a way of revealing the import of Existence (e), it must be practiced as a religion, whereas in religious ceremonial (f) there need be no such practice involved. Similarly, when art is offered up to God (d), it must first be created as a secular product, whereas in the case of religious art (g) the work from the very beginning is concerned with God. From a religious standpoint, religion treated as a way of revealing the import of Existence (e)—liturgical art—is more important and precious than art offered to God (d)—consecrated art. From the standpoint of art, religious ceremonial (f) and religious art (g) have a preferential status. Art takes consecrated art to be art and nothing more and finds liturgical art to have a rather limited value.

For both religion and art, then, religious art has value, the one seeing it as inferior to pure religion but superior to any other form or use of art, the other seeing it as a sub-species of art, art made subject to special conditions. It deserves to be made central. The examination of (d) consecrated art, (e) liturgical art, and (f) religious ceremonial can wait until religious art has been examined in some detail.

(g) A work of art is a created product. It unites the emotions with a prospect and a resistant medium, thereby at once embodying and representing existing space, time, or becoming. Religious art is art because it embodies and points to one of these dimensions of Existence; it is religious because it also embodies and points to God. It does both because it deals with both Existence and God. Existence is here primary; God is not faced directly but only in the form of a qualification of Existence. Religious art is therefore an object of suspicion on the part of some religious men.

The Puritans had a point when they took sharp exception to art, religious no less than the secular, though even they took note of art in their language, songs, and buildings. Religious art, because it tempts one to neglect pure art, also tends to become the work of mere craftsmen, engaged in education or propaganda. Artists frequently resist the lure of religious art, though no one can altogether escape it, since it is deeply imbedded in our traditions, culture, and myths.

I have elsewhere dealt in some detail both with the main problems of art and the main branches into which it can be divided. I have discussed nine arts at some length—architecture, sculpture, painting (which I take to be arts primarily concerned with portraying space); musical composition, story, and poetry (which I take to be arts primarily concerned with creating time); and musical performance, theatre, and dance (which I take to be arts primarily concerned with re-presenting process). I will now follow the lead of that discussion, using its conclusions regarding the nature of each of these arts as a basis for understanding the related religious arts.

1) Architecture is the art of bounding space. Religious architecture is the art of bounding a space which has been divinely affected either as a whole or in some limited part. The space in both cases is creatively reproduced by the architect. He captures the texture and communicates its nature, via the emotions. When the religious architect attends to some special site or orientation he concentrates on God as making a signal difference to a limited part of space. When he attends to the whole of space he takes account of God as an omnipresent, unifying being.

Orientation can be physical or symbolic. In the former case one is turned toward the rising sun, the sky, some sacred place, or even, as Scully has brilliantly argued in relation to the Greek temples, toward the horned or clefted mountains. In these cases the distant boundaries offer physical limits whose structure, common meaning, and association refer to God as involved with some portion of space. A purely symbolic orientation is given when the building is pointed toward a remote place, such as Mecca or Jerusalem. Such orientation is, strictly speaking, not architectural, for these distant places do not define the environment of the building.

An environment lies between the limits of the building and a distant boundary. That environment can have an importance greater than or equal to that of the building or its interior. Most often though, the environment is one shared by secular groups. When this is the case it has both a secular and a religious meaning. It is sacred only for those who see it from the vantage point of the religious building, who see it as a place where processions can begin or end or where various religious rites can be performed.

Orientations in modern cities are usually beyond the control of architects; these must usually be content with symbolic orientations. Environments too are beyond the architects' determinations; as a result, they must therefore usually be content either with a limited environment in which the building is placed, or with whatever environment the community allows it to have. One can rarely control more in a religious building than its boundaries, voids, and enclosed spaces. In the absence of a controlled environment, the walls and roofs could express the nature of the needed orientations, thereby giving physical shape to the orientation point. The columns of the Greek temple, the flying buttresses of the medieval cathedral, the simple wooden white churches of the low church Protestants, the figures on the southern Indian temples are attempts in this direction. Today, when there is a serious effort being made to produce fresh architecture for various religious groups, the architect must discover ways of making evident in his exterior walls the orientation and environment which, in ideal circumstances, would have been physically exhibited.

Windows and doors are voids relating the interior of a building to the environment, and the environment to the building. In the absence of a controlled environment, they can function only with respect to the circumambient light and air. Placing the windows properly will, however, enable one to make use of the light and air in such a way as to sharpen the impact and import of the exterior world. When light streaming in through the skylight or strained through stained windows is made to fall on dramatic places within the interior or at certain times, the manageable values of orientation and environment are imposed on the interior, and there need be no reference made to the outside. This is particularly true in modern times. The modern place of worship is a closed-off place, defining an area whose doors and windows are entrance ways for either limited parts of or for the whole of a God-affected space. In the case of the Hebrews, Hindus, and the Muslims, where there are no stained windows or carved doors, there is no mediation of the divine in the passage ways, entrances, and the like. A localized or an omnipresent being is nevertheless exhibited in the contouring of the space or in the nature and location of particular subdivisions of it, such as altar, minaret, pulpit, or shrine.

Architecture makes use of a four-fold scale—physical, qualitative, emotional, and social. These have modified forms in religious architecture. A physical scale is quantitative, relating to man's size, the fact that his size is to be framed in the whole architectural space, and that he will interplay with what takes place there. An attempt on the part of religious architects to make evident the immensity of God will lead to deliberate contrasting of the size of man and the magnitude of the interior space. But this contrast must be achieved without denying the fact that the space will have to be subdivided and contoured to accommodate actual men. A qualitative scale relates to the spiritual import of the created space. Its use enables us to recognize that man has a distinctive promise, to be realized in that space in a special way. The religious architect sees that promise to involve a final assessment of man by God. He tries therefore to dramatize the space, to make it come to a focus in a limited region which epitomizes the climactic meaning of that final assessment. An emotional scale reflects a man's private interests. The religious architect treats this scale as primarily relating to the participation of men in the religious community, with its consequent bearing on them as individuals. Architectural space should also be measured in social terms, as providing places for the activities of a number of men. The religious architect makes use of a social scale to promote the solidarity of the religious community, and the conjoint functioning of its members.

These scales, though primarily used on the inside space, also have relevance to the solid space of the walls and grounds, and to the environmental space connecting the outside of the building with the distant boundary. Each one of the scales could have a primary role, with the others subservient. A chapel raises problems which relate primarily to a qualitative space; a cathedral and a temple raise problems which relate primarily to a quantitative and a social scale; a synagogue, a mosque, a local church are scaled primarily emotionally and socially. In none of these cases are the other scales neglected, but they do not get to the essence of the works.

Architectural scales have no unit measures. They are not repetitively used, and have no reality except so far as they are embodied in the space. Their nature and use are created in the creating of the space, and can be discerned only by one who looks at the space as a created product. Not even the physical scale can be seen in any other way. Just as the metronome will provide beats but will not help with the melody, so rulers will give one numbers, not scaled magnitudes.

2) *Sculpture:* A sculptured object has a two-fold scale. The sculptor ignores the social use which is so essential to an architectural work; he also ignores the physical scale in terms of which the magnitude is to be related to the average size of man. Instead he concentrates on the spiritual import and the private emotional values of the work.

A piece of sculpture occupies an area. It has no empty spaces to contour. All its holes and recesses are part of it as a single voluminous object, completely solid. They are agencies for geometrizing a space in a powerful way so that every part is effective on all the others through the body of the work and over the surface. The sculpture has no necessary location, though it can define a site and an interior space, or can be made to point to some distant and desirable object. Surrounded by a spectator space of endless plasticity, it can in theory be viewed from any angle, position, or distance.

In religious sculpture the nature of a limited part of a divinely qualified space is represented. Religious sculptures differ from one another, depending on the different degrees of stress they give to the role of God. When they portray a religious being or activity, they risk a loss of the divine component. Muslims, Jews, and low church Protestants are acutely aware of the danger. They resolutely resist the temptation to picture and thereby risk making an idol of God. They restrict their sculpting to candelabras, minarets, gardens, and the like. The multiplicity of arms and legs, and the use of animal heads for the Gods help the Hindu to escape idolatry by a different route. The medieval sculptor found the same answer through the use of grotesques and exaggerations of familiar religious images.

Different religions can be characterized as epitomizing some such basic attitude as compassion, love, obedience, or as being occupied with the sanctification of such archetypal occurrences as birth and death, union and separation. Religious sculptors express these under the guidance of a religious creed or myth, and in a work which embodies and represents a divinely qualified spatial Existence.

God is a spiritual being, tremendous and absolute, adumbratively apprehended. His infinite and irreducible import can be conveyed even in finite material. This is what religious sculpture does. It reveals God's great magnitude and majesty by making a work which represents space as possessed of a single value—or, what is the same thing, which shows that God is omnipresent. God can of course be said to prefer one place over another at various times. The sculptor who is interested in this fact will concern himself with the depiction of particular occurrences assumed to take place in the preferred spots. Those occurrences, for the religious sculptor, will not deny God's omnipresence, but instead will stress the fact that His omnipresence is being expressed in a distinctive way in a distinctive place.

Not all that a sculpture can portray need occur in space. Events on Olympus, in paradise, in heaven or hell, the activities of disembodied spirits, are not locatable in actual space. But all of them can be treated as providing opportunities for the sculptor to present us with spatialized light and darkness. Indeed, there is perhaps no better way to read a religious sculpture than to take it to convey to us the nature of a divinely determined spatialized cosmos of light and darkness. Each work in a different way shows the nature of a struggle between light and darkness, not as equal forces or ultimate realities, but as primary expressions of a divinely affected space. Not altogether separable from the exhibition of light and darkness in this sense is the exhibition of fluidity and stability, manifested in part by the play of light, and in part by the bleeding of the different forms and curves and themes into one another. Modern mobiles can be most effectively used for such portrayal, if the fluidity be balanced by a stability, and the whole be recognized to epitomize an omnipresent being, infinitely malleable in space.

To do justice to the infinitude of God and the divisibility of space, a religious sculpture should be endlessly articulated without losing its unity. A combination of all three—light and darkness, fluidity and stability, unity and divisibility—is needed if there is to be an ideal sculptural religious work. And they are perhaps most readily united if the religious sculpture does not too readily assume the role of a sign of some familiar image or story. There is a place for the story but this should be subordinated to the work of showing how God is present in space.

3) *Painting:* The one religious art which seems to have interested most artists and spectators is painting, particularly in the West, beginning with the Renaissance. We have almost countless paintings of the Magi, the Crucifixion, the Assumption; almost every story in the Bible has been painted from many angles. Different figures and events have so often been portrayed that a well-defined set of symbols of them—lamb, bird, ring, key—have come into common use. The fact that religious objects or events are portrayed, or that the painting is produced under the auspices of a church or on a religious occasion does not suffice to take the painting out of the class of secular works, or of consecrated ones. A religious painting must embody and point to God as involved with space, and thus as making a difference to it, in whole or part—and this few paintings do. Painting has not often been pursued as a religious art.

Painting is the art of making space visible. It has something of the texture, and makes evident to us the nature of the existent space, which is outside but yet relevant to us. Using colors and shapes to make the space visible, and utilizing various cues to enable others to read it, it encompasses a plurality of directions, planes, themes, and stresses. Vital and pulsative, it has a rationale whose qualitative tonality must be experienced to be known. It need not reproduce any familiar object; familiar objects will in fact often make one miss the underlying reality which the painting is to exhibit. It has neither environment nor spectator areas, since to appreciate it one must enter it, not see it as being at a distance—though one must, to be sure, be at a distance from it to look at it. To see it one must give oneself to its structure, live through its pattern, be in it, and this by following the lead of the feelings which have been aroused by it.

Religious painting makes visible an existent space which has been affected by God. The very embodiment of an endlessly malleable light, the religious painting is articulated by what is comparatively dark, divisible, and stable. From this it would appear that modern abstract painting should prove to be singularly appropriate for religious art, provided that the painter, no less than the spectator, makes the work reveal and point to God as omnipresent.

4) *Musical Composition:* Musical composers are masters of the art of creating time. The sensuous, silent, metrical, melodic, rhythmic totality which they produce reveals Existence to be ominous and benign, coming to be and passing away inside a single whole whose beginning and ending are internally defined. Were such a composer to concern himself with the texture and import of a divinely controlled time, he would produce a religious work in which God is revealed to be omniscient, that is, to encompass all past and future time. The composition is not limited to the use of a particular structure or instrument. It need not have the form of a hymn or psalm, fugue or symphony, chant or community song, make use of voice, organ, or

harp. But it must redefine the entire future and past, give them a meaning which they did not have before. Religious time passes away and yet abides in the form of presents which redefine the past and future. These presents are kairotic moments, places where eternity unites with time.

5) *Religious Literature:* Religious language fills out the time created in the formation of kairotic moments. It may speak of humdrum things; it may indulge in gnomic expressions; it can take the form of parables, myths, stories, dramatic situations; it may have a tragic or a comic motif. But it must exhibit the presence of God in itself and in the temporal Existence outside. In that language the kairotic moments not only define antecedents and consequences, but affect these, press on them at different rates and in different ways.

The language of the Bible, the Gospels, the Koran, Sutras, and other scriptures can be treated as sacramental (b), consecrated (d), or religious (g). If the first, these works are to be read with reverence as embodying God; if the second they are to be viewed as means by which to become one with God as outside and beyond time; if the third they are to be lived with both as embodying God Himself, and as pointing to Him as already embodied in the world beyond. But only when they are the third, and thus only when they are read as religious works can they be said to be forms of art which convey the commands, the injunctions, the intent of God—His "message."

Like all other literature, religious writings have their own grammar, rationale, vocabulary. Religion speaks with a clarity and precision within its own domain. To be sure it starts with the language of every day, and whatever it says never loses reference to the meanings and even objects of every day. But its syntax is its own. It refers to its proper object but only for those who accede to its syntactical demands. He who belonged to some one religion, or who looked at his own as an object to investigate, could write and tell a story pertinent to some other religion, providing he makes evident that the story does refer us to Existence as already affected by God.

Religious language has its own rules. This makes it possible for the innocent and inexperienced to enter into the religion and make use of its language more readily than others—and yet miss its basic import. Not being caught in other languages as thoroughly as habituated adults, it is easier for them to accept the way in which the language is to be used; not having the insight of the adult, not aware of the resistant material of daily life with which they have to work in order to get the full power of the new language, they slip quickly from point to point, not understanding what is said. Conversely, the language of a religion can be used as a daily language. It can even be used to express antireligious sentiments. When this is done the overtones and affiliations characteristic of the language in the religion are neglected, and its grammar and vocabulary become so far indistinguishable from the grammar and vocabulary of daily life. This is one of the reasons why in Israel today the orthodox

Jews refuse to use the Hebrew of the Bible for everyday affairs. They, it can be rightly said, are the only Jews who insist on living in a Ghetto and speaking Yiddish there.

A similar issue is raised by the attempt to "demythologize" the Bible, which is to say, to free it from all reference to actual occurrences in history and to interpret it in terms of Existentialism. But where the orthodox Jews in Israel think that a religious language can have no proper secular use, the demythologizers suppose that no literature can be clearly, obtrusively religious. They view the stories of the Bible as tales purporting to be historic, overlaying a more basic religious message. But the tales also purport to carry a religious message, and on their surface.

If the story of Cain and Abel is treated as religious, it is not taken to be an historic event—though there could have been such an event and this could have been the origin and inescapable reference of the biblical story. Nor is it to be viewed as a metaphor or a popularization of the struggle of Good and Evil. It is to be read as making evident the nature of a divinely controlled time. If we abstract from its characters, incidents, "plot," and climax, we will lose an immediate apprehension of the emotional import of the fact that God is omniscient, a being who brings the present and past together in the present.

The story of the Crucifixion may or may not be historic; that is a matter for historians to determine. It may express a message to be understood only by the faithful; that is a matter for a believer to determine. What remains true, regardless of what these decide, is a story which vividly expresses the nature of a divinely controlled, objective time, a time which cannot be fully grasped in its vitality and dramatic import by any demythologizer. Demythologizing gives one the philosophic import but not the meaning, not the depth, the texture, the emotional value of the occurrence.

A religious story is to be distinguished from the kind that can be told in a Sunday school, or repeated or reported in a history of religions. It does not offer something for scientific investigation. It presents us with a created work, complete in itself, in which and with which one can live, and thereby be enabled to move through it and beyond it into a world outside. It has a texture, not of a mere existential time, but of one which is unified, which encompasses in signal presents the omniscient nature of God. God redefines time, not by controlling its flow or making selections from or additions to it, but by taking up that time into a new context and a new unity. It is this transposed and transformed time which is conveyed in a religious story.

Stories make evident the tragedy and comedy latent in the world beyond. In tragedy we become aware that Existence is ruthless, impersonal, destructive of our values. In comedy we become aware that Existence has a value transcending the arbitrary limited values which we impose on it, as individuals and as members of some society. The two are never wholly separable. There can be no religious comedy, no Divine Comedy, without a Divine Tragedy. Though there is confidence in most religions that the good will conquer evil, and thus that "comedy" will eventually be the outcome, there is religious tragedy even for an optimistic religion, such as Christianity. The awareness that Existence is tragic, even when under the aegis of God, is what most of the stories in the Bible in fact reveal, and which it is the intent of the Gospels in part to balance with an account of a triumphant rebirth elsewhere.

Throughout the history of religion one finds burlesques, farces, buffoonery, serving good ends. They provide relief in solemn periods, punctuate sombre events, mark the beginning or ending of sad occasions. Comedy here is a form of therapy. Comedy can also have a distinctive artistic role in religion. Even the most deeply religious of men is feeble and fallible, exhibiting multiple false values and evaluations from which he ought to be stripped. To see him stripped of these in the ordinary course of daily life is to share in a daily comedy; to see him stripped of these by virtue of the activity of a divinely qualified Existence is to watch a deeper and more vital comedy.

Existence can be mediated by anything. Its operation is most evident, however, when mediated through the innocent, for these are closer in spirit to it than are conventional men. To enjoy a comedy one identifies oneself with the operation of Existence, and thereby becomes vicariously purged of his follies—and incidentally (as is the case with all art) has his emotions purged by having them expressed in a controlled and satisfying way.

The men who are affected and the agent through whom the actions and purgations occur in both comedy and tragedy need not be free men. There need be no exercise of choice. The follies of mankind, the impersonality of Existence have no necessary connection with evil intent, knowledge, or will. Freedom merely makes all action more poignant. But men, regardless of what they freely desire or do, are everywhere pretentious, needing the correction of comedy, and are everywhere feeble, suffering the onslaughts of a ruthless Existence, to be portrayed in a tragedy.

A story is self-contained. It has its own themes, development, climax. The characters it portrays are what they are revealed to be in the story. That they may have some existence outside, that the story purports to be true or to recapture what had happened, may be a fact, but what we know from the story is what we are told by it. The fundamentalist who reads the Bible as the "literal" truth is then in a sense right over against those who follow the "higher criticism." Unfortunately, he slips rather readily into the supposition that the story relates to something occurring in the secular world, although his actual reading and understanding belie his own interpretations.

What is revealed is something outside the frame of the story. It could be an occurrence in history, but if so it is in a history which makes use of a divinely qualified Existence. It is not an occurrence in secular history, the history which makes use of a nonqualified Existence. When the fundamentalist dismisses the latter form of

Existence, and the secular history which it makes possible, he but balances the equally unwarranted dogmatism of the secular historian who dismisses the fundamentalist's outlook in the same off-hand way.

6) *Poetry:* Poetic language is distinct from the language of story, sometimes in vocabulary and always in syntax, use, and substance. It need not be put in verse; it may abjure metaphor, it can tell a story, and it can even include areas of prosaic description. Its language is newly created and as self-contained as the specialized colors of a painting are. Commonsense language is a subordinated component in it, and offers a counterthrust for it. An articulated whole of time, epitomizing whatever time there might be outside, before, or after it, it is unitary and diversified, constant and changing. In it words are affiliated by sound and meaning, not by plot or truth, logic or argument, revealing time to be corrosive and sustaining, with varying thicknesses and turns.

Religious poetry deals with omniscience compressed within a single moment.

It subjects this to a creative verbalization, thereby producing a distinctive time. This time, in contrast with the kairotic which unites eternity with daily time, is freshly made by the poet, though answering to a time outside. A religious poem is a full-bodied rhythmic whole in which God is present. It expands and contracts line by line, sound by sound, meaning by meaning at the same time that it is structured and confined. Without denying it its corrosive, transitory character, this time is fixated, stabilized. The divine unity in the poem enables the poem to present and to point to a limited temporal Existence, qualified by God.

The ostensible topic of a religious poem could be a gravestone, flowers, sunlight, sickness, winter, war—anything. If "symbol" be understood to relate to a divinely affected content which is enjoyed and which directs us to a divinely affected content beyond it, all religious art can be said to be symbolic. But it is to be noted that the referent of religious art is not God, but Existence as affected by Him.

Religious poetry presents in a distinctive moment the texture and meaning of a divinely qualified temporal Existence. We recognize such poetry most readily when distinctive types of metaphor are used. One type links the native abilities of nondivine things with roles, privileges, endowments, promises, duties having their source in God. Another type starts with some divine ability and links this with some worldly roles. We use the one when we say that a man is "God's servant"; we use the other when we speak of "God, the father." In both we presuppose that "God" has a literal meaning, for a metaphor is built out of terms having nonmetaphoric roles.

As has already been observed, it is not necessary to use metaphors in a poem. In the ordinary course of poetic discourse a metaphor serves to interrelate meanings which are normally treated as independent and contrastive—those which refer to animals and men, men and women, the living and the nonliving, and the like. The metaphor results when these independent, sharply contrasted items are made to illuminate one another. To say of a man that he is timid, soft-spoken, sensitive and the like is to speak literally; to say of him that he is womanly is to speak metaphorically. The metaphor in a religious poem also uses independent and contrasted items to illuminate one another, but concentrates on the use of terms which refer to man and a divinely tinged Existence, even when apparently speaking only of love or dogs or tigers. All religious art can be said to be metaphoric in this sense, for all express the way man and a temporalized omniscience affect one another.

The poetry of meditation and so-called metaphysical poetry are no more appropriate or inappropriate to religion than any other type. A poet can select any theme, follow any method, use any form of expression, and speak of any topic, and still be writing religious poetry, so long as he exhibits and points to a divinely tinged time.

Is it possible for a nonreligious man to write religious poetry? This question is but another form of a question which has come before us before in connection with other arts. Since a nonreligious man cannot, except accidentally, use his words in such a way as to portray a reality which a religious man discerned, anyone who read his poem and grasped something of God from it, would be doing something legitimate, but which, because it is not controlled by, is not justly attributable to the poem.

We usually need cues in the form of familiar metaphors and allusions to enable us to discern the religious nature of a poem, but strictly speaking, this is not necessary. The fact can be discovered by noting that the poem has a unity in addition to the one the poet provides. The religious poem is inseparable from the objective unity of God and Existence. This unity the religious poet creatively combines with the time of the poem.

7) *Religious Music:* The arts of music, theatre, and dance have often been combined. There is some plausibility in the idea that they were initially intertwined, particularly in religious situations. What-

ever their origin and interplay, however, they are pursued today by different artists. And they have distinctive problems, though all of them are concerned with the creative expression of the texture and meaning of a genuine process of becoming, whose nature is revealed in the very process of enjoying the created work. Each makes use of the vitality of the artist to produce a work which is voluminous, encompassing, within which the artist himself will be found. Music creates an assertive, the theatre a maturating, and the dance a self-maintaining force, each with its own peculiar way of filling out a volume in multiple ways and from multiple directions.

A musical performance, the production of a unified totality of tones of dynamic power severally and together, differs from a musical composition as becoming does from time, volume from a line, the heard from the seen, the common from the personal. It is a solid tissue of sounds and silences, each having its own power and integrity, while allowing for the presence of the others. Each sound comes as it were from a distance while occupying the entire volume. Each has a distinctive centre of gravity, and all of them environ the listener. The whole is a complex of sounds and silences filling out the same area, but coming from different places at different rates and with different effects. It reveals Existence to have heights and depths, with newly created starting points and termini, powerful and causal.

Religious music need not make reference to any religious topic or have a title which says anything having to do with religion. It need not be used by a religious group, nor be composed or performed by one who already accepts the religion which makes use of it. Nor must it be thought of as having a place inside some religious ceremony. It need not be solemn. It need not have a composition prepared for it. Concerned with capturing the texture and the import of an existential becoming which is qualified by God, it exhibits Him primarily not as omnipresent or omniscient —the task of the spatial and temporal arts —but as omnipotent.

The Buddhists and Hindus seek a peace in the bosom of an absolute and ultimate reality. If they wish to make use of art, they must deal with that reality as involved with Existence, reveal what the result imports for a "suffering" world. Their tendency though is to make use of art as essentially referential, to point to the reality as beyond all distinctions. Their music, like their Buddhas and Sivas, has a power which a strictly religious art does not. But it is the power of a consecrated, not of a religious art. Clear signs can sometimes be more effective than poorly produced religious art objects.

Existence can be benign or malevolent, sustaining or destructive. Religious music is concerned with it as more than and other than either of these. Through a controlled use of sounds and silences it reveals a unifying, focussed, transcending power—a flexible, conserving free being which is vitally present in us, in the music, and in the Existence beyond both us and the music.

Musical composition and musical performance are sometimes related as model to copy, creation to craftsmanship, text to interpretation. But the fact that they concern themselves with different dimensions of Existence—time and becoming—points up their difference. And when we turn to religious musical compositions and performances their difference can be quite striking. A musical religious composition can be played by anyone. It could be played with feeling and imagination, and still yield only a secular work of art. On the other hand, a secular composition could be played by one in a religious spirit. The composition would then evidently be used as material to be transformed inside a religiously-toned performance. Such use of material is but a signal illustration of what all performances do—use the composition as material to be quickened in a different art.

The effect that omnipotence has on the dynamics of Existence can be made the object of reflection in philosophy, theology, and cosmology. But none of these conveys the import of that effect on man, in such a way that he is able to grasp it emotionally. And there is no better way of exhibiting the overall meaning of the effect than through a musical performance in which the music environs, moves in and through the listener as the very epitomization of a cosmic and ultimately saving power. The musician's technique here will be indistinguishable from that which he exhibits in a secular situation. He will read the composition with the same imagination with which he reads any other. But he will differ in the kind of dynamism he will seek to embody and make evident in the different situations. In a religious performance there will be stresses and variations which would be absent were the same piece played in order to make evident the nature of Existence as such, and not Existence as qualified by an omnipotent God. The result might be inferior to what he might otherwise have produced. A secularized performance of what might have been religious may be aesthetically superior to the latter, not because it makes more ready provision for the presence of excellence, but because it is more within the competence of the musician.

He who would produce religious works will do so, as a rule, only if he starts with a well-developed religious temper, trained and directed by some organized religion. Religious music, like other religious works, are usually the products of men who are members of some established religion. They carry over into their work the worshipful attitude which they exhibit in their prayers and other religious acts. The work they produce, as a consequence, represents the religion in a new context. But a religious work of art has a religious dimension which may have no counterpart in any other religious context. It may be forged then and there as the artist works over material in the effort to iconize a vital Existence controlled by omnipotence. This requires an activity which is like that of religious conversion, but produced by working in and through recalcitrant material.

There are men, apparently, who become most religious when engaged in the making of a work of art, and particularly music. It is not that they are devoted to their work—one can be devoted to the task of producing mischief. They are religious because and so far as their work is religious, and this is religious only so far as it creatively reproduces an omnipotently controlled existential process and reveals its import for man.

8) *Theatre:* The particular location that a theatrical performance might have in our daily world is irrelevant to the being or nature of that performance. The performance is dislocated from every external setting; it occurs when and where it is performed, to make evident the nature of a maturating causality. A performance is a self-sufficient totality in which the meanings, gestures, characters, plot are entirely inside, spaced by substantial silences and rests, moving along at its own pace, and producing in its own way what follows, thereby portraying an Existence which comes to expression in multiple interlocked channels.

A religious theatrical performance, since it is a theatrical performance, need not therefore be produced inside a church. Nor need it deal with any religious topic or be consciously designed with religion in mind. It exhibits a vital diversified becoming as affected by an omnipotent unitary God. It makes evident what such existential omnipotence means for man, what men are like as interlocked with it, and what it is like as standing outside them. It shows us man struggling against, being supported by, defying and being transformed by Existence as the agency of omnipotence.

What a church does with respect to God, the religious play does with respect to Existence as qualified by God. It is no substitute for a church, no supplement for it. It is not to be identified with the liturgy, with church services, no matter how dramatic these be. The services in a church might of course be dramatic, with a definite climax and a clear beginning and ending, but they are not theatre. One who came to the service from the outside, and looked at the whole as a member of an audience, still would not see a play, for there would be no characters involved, no interplay of incidents to define the development of a plot. The most he could see would be a mirroring or a procession or a ceremony, having turns and stresses, moments of preparation, turning point, and terminus. He would not live with it, and would not become aware of the reality which the participants in the service were coming to know. The participants in a religious service, like the audience in a genuine play, become alert to the nature of a reality outside themselves. But the participants in the service (and this whether they be leaders or followers) are like actors without an audience, and thus like actors in a rehearsal and not in a genuine performance. They are working through something rather than creatively making it. They go through states for the sake of what is to be represented rather than to make something which, by its very self-sufficiency, will serve to illuminate an omnipotently controlled, diversified Existence.

In a religious theatrical performance, the characters and incidents all serve to punctuate a single fact, Existence qualified by omnipotence. The performance enables one to have an emotionally sustained acquaintance with the nature of that Existence, and to become emotionally aware of it as pertinent to man. The actors and the audience then become participants in a kind of religious activity, since they share in an embodied God and are directed to Him as outside the performance. Their experience is nevertheless unlike that which they have when they participate in the activities of a religious community, since that deals with God as He is apart from His involvement in the dynamics of Existence. A religious theatrical performance thus offers no substitute for a communal religious activity; it may even tempt one to remain outside a religious community, since it provides one not only with something like a religious experience but with an aesthetic one. Nor can it be substituted for a secular theatrical performance, for though requiring artistic creativity, it is concerned with Existence only under a decided restriction. But like all the other religious arts, it has its own integrity and its own value, competing with those contained in the secular arts and in religion.

9) *Dance:* The theatre punctuates the becoming offered by music. A dance unifies that becoming, fills it out, makes it be the lifeblood of the entire spatial volume, the floor and the air. The dance uses the human body, gravity, and the available space to constitute a new complete but revelatory dynamism in which the audience participates. It is a created organic becoming, solidified, self-contained, in which rests and movements, gestures and postures are all interlocked. A dance has its own area, time, and form of development. It tells us that a pulse of causation is endlessly plastic, having its own logic, unfolding within a self-contained time and space.

The actor creates a place within a plot-defined whole. The dancer creates a whole from an idea-defined position. The dancer vitalizes all of the dance area at the same time, though stressing some subordinate portion, whereas the actor starts with a plot and vitalizes some area which the plot demands be so vitalized. Like the sounds of music, dancers occupy a plurality of dimensions in a single volume. The dance's movements are directed backward and forward, up and down and sideways in irregular beats, and this even when they seem to point in one direction or another and to do so with regularity.

The dance tells no story; it has no plot, clarifies no characters, provides no incidents. It is essentially rhythmic, an accumulative affair, teaching us that Existence is relentless and flexible, promising good and evil.

The dance seems to have had a religious origin. It once was solely a part of a religious activity. Today it sometimes has this role, i.e., is a sacramental art. But it also has a secular form and may take the form of a religious art. The religious dance is concerned with expressing and revealing a becoming in which God is a qualifying component. It leads us to omnipotence as a now present causality, freely forming, productive, epitomizing all that had been and all that will be. Gravity is quickened by it, made to pulsate through an entire space, focussed on here and there by various bodies. When it includes nondancing components, such as sacrifices, circumcisions, processions within it, the religious dance alters their affiliations and thereby changes their import.

A religious dance, more than any other religious art, brings us in immediate contact with God as involved with Existence. The other arts have stronger referential notes; they make us more alert to the transcendent side of God. The dance, therefore, on the one side, comes closest to being a purely religious activity, and on the other, to being most distant from one, since a purely religious activity does justice both to the immanent and transcendent sides of God. Supplemented by activities which serve to direct one clearly toward God as transcendent, the religious dance could be a vital part of a religion, though it is to be noted that unlike religion it does not relate one to God except through the mediation of the Existence which He qualifies. A dance never succeeds in achieving what a religious act does—an experience of God and a reference to Him as beyond the experience and the experiencer.

A religious dance is an art. Without technique, without control, without a concern for the production of beauty, without vital creativity, it would no longer be an art, it would no longer be a religious dance. The frenzied leaps, the rolls, and twists of religious enthusiasts, therefore ought not to be termed "religious dances." At the very most they can be said to be sacramental parts of a religious activity. They are to be distinguished too from consecrated dances which, pursued as a secular art, are referred to a religious context for supplementation or transformation. The Hasid engages in sacramental dances, the Balinese dancing girls engage in secular dances which are consecrated, given a religious import. The truly religious dance, unlike these, need not have a religious setting. If it is given such a setting it is given the additional role of a consecrated art.

A complete account of religious art would require consideration of photography, film, television, musical comedy, operas, and other combinations of the arts here briefly touched upon. None of them I think raises a distinctive problem for religious art, and need not therefore detain us. But all of them, even more strikingly than the simpler arts, raise questions of blasphemy, sacrilege, immorality, and bring us to the issue of censorship. That issue does not, however, concern the nature of religious art, but only its effects, and how these effects are to be evaluated by ecclesiastical, political, and societal powers. Over against these, religious art has its own rights, just as surely as it has rights over against secular art. Unlike secular art, it faces us with a unitary Existence, an Existence which is prevented by God from becoming endlessly fractionated. Like it, it faces us with Existence as spatial, temporal, or dynamic, and thus tells us something about the brute, remorseless cosmos in which we are now a part.

Each work of art portrays and reveals the nature and course of Existence. That is why we can learn from art. That is why we are purged by art. That is why we gain an insight into the threat and promise of Existence when we attend to art. Existence, however, is fluid, divisive, and immense. We can never lay hold of more than a fragment, and can portray it well only through the mediation of familiar cues. At best we obtain only a somewhat inchoate impression of what it imports. The value of religious art is that it enables us to grasp Existence as unified, controlled. It is to be found in communities which have no secular arts, for man is aware of Existence from the start as governed by an eternal force which he terms luck, fate, spirit. To get a secular art he must move to the stage where he can embody and portray Existence itself.

VI

d) All things are equally remote from God. To pick out any one to be consecrated is always arbitrary. And yet all are equally worthy of being consecrated, though they all do not image him equally well. And some do not fit in with man's traditions, practices, beliefs, and usages. Not all therefore are equally suitable for consecrational purposes. The arts, though, since they at once exhibit man at his creative best, embody beauty, and illuminate the nature of a basic reality, are most appropriate. They are better offerings than the choicest of fruits and cattle, since they are more certainly man's, and though not more wondrously, are more deliberately made. In offering them, man offers a most intimate, vital expression of himself and the kind of reality which most concerns him. He could, as was observed, consecrate a religious art, but he would not then be offering an art which was as pure or free as a purely secularly produced work can be.

By consecrating a secular art, man enables it to be ennobled. The consecration can occur in privacy or in public. A public consecration occurs within the confines and follows the lead of some communal religious practice. A private consecration is part of an act of devotion. It begins as an act of faith, and terminates in the submission of oneself and one's work to God for final assessment. No one knows exactly how the offering will be qualified when it is subject to divine evaluation. There was nothing wrong, so far as we know, with what Cain offered as a sacrifice. The decision not to accept it was presumably based not on the nature of the objects consecrated but on the nature of the spirit in which they were offered. It may well be that works of art are acceptable to God only so far as they are offered in a full, good faith. Consecration, however, is a human act, and one can engage in it even though what is consecrated is not accepted.

e) Liturgical art uses religious material creatively, and thereby beautifies it. The material serves not to make one acquainted with God, but to clarify the nature of Existence. However, it can be brought back into a religious context, thereby providing one with a religious act or object that has been aesthetically enhanced. And this is apparently how the liturgical arts in the current liturgical revival of the Catholic

Church are treated. Only certain kinds of objects and activities can there be employed, since only some are initially part of its ritual and capable of being replaced there after having been dealt with as material in a creative work of art. Some objects and activities, which had a religious role, may lose this precisely because they are so enhanced aesthetically that they inhibit rather than promote religious activity. Church authorities must always look beyond a work of liturgical art to see if it can once again become a sacramental one. If it cannot, it cannot be endorsed by them.

f) *Ceremonial:* Religion, strictly speaking, is not possible without faith. And faith requires the presence of God in men in such a way as to point to Him as apart from them, and all else. What is sometimes called "natural religion" relates not to God alone, but to God as qualified by Existence. God, from this point of view, is the unitary essence of a spatio-temporal dynamic cosmos. The Stoics, Spinoza, and perhaps Hegel think of God in somewhat these terms. God is not taken by them to be wholly immanent. His unity is seen to transcend the realm of Existence. But it is a qualified unity, a unity which has been extensionalized.

A natural religion is a special type of religion. It may come to expression in the worship of natural objects, but there is no need that this occur. Natural objects could be used as signs or occasions, but even this is not necessary. A natural religion could be privately pursued and come to no public expression. If it is publicly expressed it could take any number of forms and be backed by any number of theologies. Taoism and Confucianism, and certain varieties of Japanese Buddhism, seem to offer different varieties of such a natural religion. They make evident that natural religion should not be equated with superstition or irreligion, as is sometimes done.

A religious ceremonial has a sacramental status with other acts and objects inside a religion. It could be made the topic of a religious art. It can also be taken to constitute the entire substance of the public expression of a religion. It then becomes the vehicle for a natural religion. God will be present in that vehicle and will be referred to by means of it, but it will be God as qualified by Existence. The ceremonial will, then, in its limited spatial, temporal, and vital character, mirror the nature of that God. One could participate in the ceremonial without becoming aware of Him. The ceremonial will then be nothing more than a spectacle, a form of theatre when this has lost the status of an art. But he who participated in the ceremonial with a faith in a God of natural religion would achieve something similar to what he would achieve were he engaged in an art. He would capture something of the texture of Existence, and would be aware of its power, but of course only so far as it was a component of his faith. He would not get to pure Existence. To do that he would have to practice or participate in an art. Nor would he have any inkling as to what Existence might import for him as an emotional being in a cosmic setting. He would be aware only of its import for and through God.

Just as a religious art, while exhibiting the essentials of art, tells us something about God, so a religious ceremonial, while exhibiting the essentials of a religion, tells us something about Existence. He who is interested primarily in portraying Existence or in reaching God will look askance at both. Religious art offers only a qualified art, and religious ceremonial offers us only a qualified religion.

If we wish to grasp the nature of pure Existence and see what this imports for man, we can do nothing better than practice a secular art. If we wish to reach God we can do nothing better than be religious. If we wish to grasp the nature of God as mediated by Existence, we must practice a religious art. If we wish to grasp the nature of Existence as mediated by God we must share in a religious ceremonial. There are still other things to do. Men are, after all, obligated to realize an Ideal Good and ought to make proper use of their minds. And since God and Existence mediate and are mediated by the Ideal and the categories of knowledge, the enterprises of ethics and knowledge should be intersected by religion and art to yield entirely new areas where men are and should also be vitally involved.

The Aquinas Lectures

Published by the Marquette University Press,
Milwaukee 3, Wisconsin

St. Thomas and the Life of Learning (1937) by Fr. John F. McCormick, S.J., professor of philosophy, Loyola University.

St. Thomas and the Gentiles (1938) by Mortimer J. Adler, Ph.D., director of the Institute of Philosophical Research, San Francisco, Calif.

St. Thomas and the Greeks (1939) by Anton C. Pegis, Ph.D., professor of philosophy, Pontifical Institute of Mediaeval Studies, Toronto.

The Nature and Functions of Authority (1940) by Yves Simon, Ph.D., professor of philosophy of social thought, University of Chicago.

St. Thomas and Analogy (1941) by Fr. Gerald B. Phelan, Ph.D., professor of philosophy, St. Michael's College, Toronto.

St. Thomas and the Problem of Evil (1942) by Jacques Maritain, Ph.D., professor *emeritus* of philosophy, Princeton University.

Humanism and Theology (1943) by Werner Jaeger, Ph.D., Litt.D., University professor, Harvard University.

The Nature and Origins of Scientism (1944) by John Wellmuth.

Cicero in the Courtroom of St. Thomas Aquinas (1945) by E. K. Rand, Ph.D., Litt.D., LL.D., Pope professor of Latin, *emeritus,* Harvard University.

St. Thomas and Epistemology (1946) by Fr. Louis-Marie Regis, O.P., Th.L., Ph.D., director of the Albert the Great Institute of Mediaeval Studies, University of Montreal.

St. Thomas and the Greek Moralists (1947, Spring) by Vernon J. Bourke, Ph.D., professor of philosophy, St. Louis University, St. Louis, Missouri.

History of Philosophy and Philosophical Education (1947, Fall) by Étienne Gilson of the *Académie française,* director of studies and professor of the history of Mediaeval philosophy, Pontifical Institute of Mediaeval Studies, Toronto.

The Natural Desire for God (1948) by Fr. William R. O'Connor, S.T.L., Ph.D., professor of dogmatic theology, St. Joseph's Seminary, Dunwoodie, N.Y.

St. Thomas and the World State (1949) by Robert M. Hutchins, Chancellor of the University of Chicago.

Method in Metaphysics (1950) by Fr. Robert J. Henle, S.J., dean of the graduate school, St. Louis University, St. Louis, Missouri.

Wisdom and Love in St. Thomas Aquinas (1951) by Étienne Gilson of the *Académie française*, director of studies and professor of the history of Mediaeval philosophy, Pontifical Institute of Mediaeval Studies, Toronto.

The Good in Existential Metaphysics (1952) by Elizabeth G. Salmon, associate professor of philosophy in the graduate school, Fordham University.

St. Thomas and the Object of Geometry (1953) by Vincent Edward Smith, Ph.D., professor of philosophy, University of Notre Dame.

Realism and Nominalism Revisited (1954) by Henry Veatch, Ph.D., professor of philosophy, Indiana University.

Imprudence in St. Thomas Aquinas (1955) by Charles J. O'Neil, Ph.D., professor of philosophy, Marquette University.

The Truth That Frees (1956) by Fr. Gerard Smith, S.J., Ph.D., professor and chairman of the department of philosophy, Marquette University.

St. Thomas and the Future of Metaphysics (1957) by Fr. Joseph Owens, C.Ss.R., associate professor of philosophy, Pontifical Institute of Mediaeval Studies, Toronto.

Thomas and the Physics of 1958: A Confrontation (1958) by Henry Margenau, Ph.D., Eugene Higgins professor of physics and natural philosophy, Yale University.

Metaphysics and Ideology (1959) by Wm. Oliver Martin, professor of philosophy, University of Rhode Island.

Language, Truth and Poetry (1960) by Victor M. Hamm, Ph.D., professor of English, Marquette University.

Metaphysics and Historicity (1961) by Emil L. Fackenheim, Ph.D., associate professor of philosophy, University of Toronto.

The Lure of Wisdom (1962) by James D. Collins, Ph.D., professor of philosophy, St. Louis University.

Religion and Art (1963) by Paul Weiss, Ph.D. Sterling Professor of philosophy, Yale University.

Uniform format, cover and binding.